EAT

MOVE

BELIEVE

For Teens

by
Malia Lewis, PhD

Illustrated by Doina Paraschiv

Published by: Eat Move Believe
Website: eatmovebelieve.org

Illustrations by: Doina Paraschiv

Manufactured in the United States.

ISBN 978-0-578-60859-4

Dedicated to teens and young men and women who face unreal challenges regarding self-esteem and body image. You are beautiful just the way you are! Believe in yourself!

Maddy

Hi, my name is Maddy and I'm a sophomore at Edison High.
I play volleyball, and I think I'm pretty good, but coach keeps bugging me to lose weight because he says I'll be quicker on the court. He's such a pain! I mean, he's OK and everything, but how am I supposed to drop weight?
I already feel ashamed of how I look. I really can't believe I'm not losing weight with the amount of time I spend working out for volleyball!

So, I've been skipping breakfast, or I just have a piece of toast if my mom is bugging me about not eating. At lunch I eat half my sandwich and toss the rest; my dad would be so mad if he knew! After school, Jenn, Lisa and I always get coffee drinks because we're so tired, but coffee doesn't have calories, right? This is just so stupid! And I'm always hungry! At dinner I pick at my food and push it around, but sometimes I'm so hungry I eat everything on my plate and then I get depressed.

How am I ever going to lose weight if I'm eating so much? Why can't I be skinny like that tiny little girl in my physics class?! I'm going to lose my mind if my parents don't quit nagging me about eating! Jenn said some lady named Ms. G is coming to school next Monday at lunch to talk about losing weight. Maybe I'll go...

Here's what she had to say...

EAT

- Have breakfast, lunch, dinner and two small snacks **EVERY DAY!**
- Eat breakfast within **one hour** of waking up.
- If you cup both hands together as if trying to hold water, the food you could hold this way represents the size of a meal for you.
- The quantity of food for a snack would be what you could hold in one cupped hand.
- If you already eat three meals a day, work on portion control and add snacks slowly.
- If you eat once or twice a day, add a meal or snack every two weeks.

- **THIS WILL TAKE TIME, SO BE PATIENT!** You are worth it!
- Eat one ingredient foods: bananas, oats, chicken, apples, nuts, rice, eggs, beans, veggies, you get the idea. Eat fresh foods!
- Also select foods that have a short list of ingredients: breads, peanut butter, yogurt, pasta, cheese, corn chips, stuff without too much added to it.
- *Avoid processed foods with a long list of ingredients you can't pronounce!*
- Download a calorie app and educate yourself about the foods you like to eat and cut down on the junk!
- Girls need **AT LEAST 1200 CALORIES PER DAY!** More if you exercise frequently.
- Boys need **AT LEAST 1800 CALORIES PER DAY!** More if you exercise frequently.

Font code:

Bold = duh! 😲

Italics = Heavy sarcasm with eye roll.

BOLD, ALL CAPS = This is kind of like your mom yelling at you, but lovingly.

- After you take out a reasonably portioned snack, **PUT THE BAG AWAY!**
- Restaurants often serve way *too much food*; **eat half and bring the rest home for later!**
- Meals should include protein, carbohydrates and fat. **WE NEED ALL THREE!**
  - In general, protein is found in meat, seafood, eggs, beans, cheese and tofu.
  - Typically, carbs are in breads, pasta, cereals, rice, fruits and veggies.
  - Fats are in butter, mayonnaise, oils and salad dressing. **Eat fats sparingly!**

- Many foods have a combination of protein, fats and carbs. Learn about foods you like.
- **Drink water!** *Soda is pure sugar* **and there's nothing about it that's good for your body!**
- Metabolism is the speed you convert food to energy for your body. **ONE OF THE WAYS TO INCREASE YOUR METABOLISM IS BY EATING SMALL, FREQUENT MEALS!**
- **YOU CAN RETRAIN YOURSELF TO LIKE HEALTHY FOODS!**
- It's OK to slip up sometimes! Forgive yourself and move on.
- Vacation, holidays or party? **DON'T CHANGE ANYTHING** and make the best choice available.
- **Avoid fast food like the plague!**
- **DON'T SNACK AFTER DINNER!**

Maddy

OMG I've been doing it all wrong! At first, I thought what Ms. G said was crazy, but I decided to follow her advice and I'm losing weight AND I feel so good! I wasn't eating enough, so I guess that made my metabolism slow down. I felt tired, grouchy and depressed, and my grades went down. Ms. G also said that working out isn't enough. You have to eat right too if you want to shed weight.

It's so weird, but to lose weight I have to eat five times a day! I have eggs and toast or oatmeal, yogurt and berries for breakfast, a turkey sandwich and fruit for lunch and a good dinner plus two snacks. I gave up sodas and coffee drinks. I guess those are full of calories and sugar, but we still get coffee drinks on Fridays. The best part is I'm NEVER hungry because I'm eating all day and I have so much energy! Volleyball practice has been way easier, my jeans are loose and, best of all, I feel so proud of myself! Who knew the way to drop weight was to eat more! Strangest of all, I am starting to like oatmeal, apples, nuts and all the other healthy stuff I'm supposed to eat.

Next, I'm going to download an app where I can look up the calories of things I like to eat. That way I can be sure to get enough calories every day. Before I was only getting about 900 calories a day, but the lady told me I need almost 2000 calories a day since I'm 15 years old and working out over two hours every day at volleyball. She told me not to get hung up on counting calories, just to educate myself so I know more about foods I like and what's healthy and what's not.

I have a lot to learn, but I'm going to keep working at it because I'm worth it! Yesterday at practice coach told me I look faster and stronger. That made me feel good, but what really makes me smile is knowing I did this for me, not anyone else! I said hi to the girl in physics. Her name is Jessica. I guess I was jealous of her because she's so tiny, and I'm not, but I realized that's not her fault and she didn't deserve my negativity toward her. My mom noticed the change in me, and now she wants to work on her eating habits too. I'm so happy my mom and I can do this together! Dad could probably benefit too!

Douglas

Hey, I'm Doug, but everybody calls me Big D. Everyone knows me, but I don't feel like I have any friends. It's kind of funny how I can be so big, yet I feel invisible.

If I'm honest, I guess I don't feel worthy of being a friend. Kids think I'm this big, dumb guy with no feelings and somehow that has rubbed off on me and now that's what I think too. I get A's in all my classes without trying, but that still doesn't make me feel good about myself. I wish I liked sports, but I just don't. The football coach has tried to get me to come out so many times, but I know I'd end up as a lineman, getting clobbered every play just to protect the quarterback. No thanks! Besides, I don't have the energy to play sports; I'm always tired.

I want to feel good about myself, like I matter to somebody. There's this girl in physics class whose name is Jessica. I wish she would look at me, just once. She's so sweet and pretty. Maybe if I could lose some weight and get a haircut, she might notice me. I saw a flyer on the school bulletin board about some lady named Ms. G, and she's coming Monday at lunch to talk about weight loss, exercise and self-esteem. Maybe I'll go…

Here's what Ms. G taught us...

MOVE

- Get regular exercise 3 to 5 days a week, **EVERY WEEK**.
- The trick is to figure out what you like to do!
- Are team sports your thing? Soccer, basketball, baseball, lacrosse, hockey, ultimate Frisbee, water polo, tennis, football, cross country, track and field?
- Do you prefer individual sports? Running, golf, walking, weight lifting, mountain biking, hiking, yoga, swimming, singles tennis, triathlons, bowling, boxing, surfing, wrestling, skiing?
- Are you competitive or do you just want to have fun?
- Do you want a work out partner or do you prefer to exercise alone?

- Answer these questions and make a plan that fits your needs and goals.
- Regular exercise helps increase your metabolism and therefore your ability to lose weight!
- **DO NOT MAKE EXCUSES; JUST GET OUT THERE AND MOVE!**
- Start your day earlier or end it later if that's what it takes to fit in exercise.
- *Regular exercise and healthy meals help prevent feeling tired during the day!*
- Work-out partners keep you accountable!

Ms. G was very knowledgeable and made me think a lot about changing things up. She talked a ton about eating small meals throughout the day and eating healthy foods. My mom is a nurse, and she always makes sure we eat well, but I decided to make my portions a little smaller and add snacks in between. Apparently, this will ramp up my metabolism and I'll burn calories more efficiently.

Ms. G also told us we need to MOVE to be healthy. After spending a few weeks deciding what I should do, I pumped up the tires on my dad's old mountain bike and went up in the hills behind our house for a ride. It was so peaceful and beautiful! I was sucking wind pretty hard at first, but after a month of regular riding I feel a lot stronger. I've even seen coyotes, snakes, tarantulas and bobcats. It's awesome out there!

My first ride was really short, but now I'm up to 15 miles! I've met a few guys I like to ride with. Some of them are better riders and push me, and sometimes I'm the one in the lead pushing the other guy. I like being helpful to other riders and feeling needed. I matter!
I also have more energy than I've had in a long time and it feels really good.

I'll always be taller than most guys, and that makes me self-conscious, but I don't need to be heavy too. I can tell I'm dropping weight because my pants are loose and that makes me feel proud. I have more work ahead to achieve my goals, but I'm determined to keep at it!

Yesterday at break I ran into Maddy from math class, and she told me I looked different. It's the first time she's ever said anything to me! I think I saw her at Ms. G's talk last month also. She's tall like me and is the star of our girls' volleyball team. Maddy looks different too, but I didn't say any thing; I will the next time I see her. For the first time in my life I feel like I have the confidence to be social! I guess I feel good about myself, like I might have something to contribute. Who knows, maybe I'll get a haircut and ask Jessica, the girl from physics, if she'd like to go on a bike ride.

Jessica

Hi, I'm Jessica, but my best friend Missy calls me Jess. I'm so scared I won't pass physics or math this year! I AM SO STUPID! Kids around me are taking notes, and they turn in all their homework. They understand the lessons, but I'm totally lost. Nothing makes sense to me. I am so dumb!

I'm embarrassed to tell my best friend that I need help because I can tell Missy understands physics. I am so pathetic! My parents are going to flip when they see my grades this semester. I don't know what I'm going to do. They think I'm getting into some fancy college, but that won't happen with the grades I have now. My stomach hurts all the time, I'm always tired and I feel so depressed.

Maybe I could drop out and go to that special high school for kids who mess up. I thought about asking Big D for help. He sits across from me and seems smart, but I don't think he likes me because he's always glaring at me. My teacher is really busy. I don't think she has time to help me, and besides, I am so far behind I'm embarrassed to ask her. She'll get mad once she realizes how lost I am, and honestly, I might cry. How can I be such a dope? I wish I was like Missy. Her biggest worry is losing 10 pounds before prom! She's making me go to some dumb weight loss thing with her tomorrow. Ugh!

At first, I didn't care about the dumb talk, but then I felt like Ms. G was talking directly to me...

Font code:

Bold = duh! 😳
Italics = Heavy sarcasm with eye roll.
BOLD, ALL CAPS = This is kind of like your mom yelling at you, but lovingly.

Believe

- **BELIEVE IN YOURSELF!**
- How do you treat yourself? Do you repeat the same negative thoughts over and over?
- I'm fat and I'm never going to lose weight!
- Nobody likes me because I don't matter.
- I'm so stupid, I'm never going to pass physics!
- What negative thoughts do you have and how can you change them to positive ones?
- **I WILL** make changes, so I feel and look healthy and strong!
- I matter, and **I WILL** feel important and loved!
- I'm good at language arts and **I WILL** get help and understand physics!
- If you tell yourself something enough times, you'll believe it, **so why not make it something positive and good?**

- Close your eyes and relax. Now think about **YOUR** negative thoughts.
- Rework those thoughts, changing them to a positive.
- Promise to repeat the positive thoughts to yourself every day - **AND BELIEVE THEM!**
- If the negative thoughts come back, simply dismiss them and shift to positive ones.
- It is **OK** to ask for help!
- Change takes time, be patient with yourself!
- **EVERYONE HAS STRUGGLES**. Don't let someone's perceived perfection fool you.
- You are unique. Avoid comparing yourself with anyone else!
- Be aware that a person's hurtful behavior toward you may be a reflection of their relationship with themselves rather than a statement about your value as a person. **DO NOT LET OTHERS BRING YOU DOWN!**
- Celebrate your strengths!

Jessica

Wow! I'm glad I went to that talk with Missy last month! First, I was shocked to see Maddy there. She's pretty, smart, popular, tall, blonde and the star of the volleyball team! What could she possibly need help with? Second, I learned that I'm probably not eating enough. I've always been thin and can eat whatever I want, so I've never paid much attention to what I eat. I added more food to breakfast, lunch and dinner, cut out a lot of the sugar I was eating and drinking, and I have way more energy! I might even start exercising, since Missy is probably going to force me to so she can lose weight.

Most important, I learned to like myself. Even though I was scared, I spoke to Ms. G about my physics and math problems. I was shaking so bad and felt like I might cry or throw up, but I figured she was a safe person to talk to. Ms. G helped me realize I should celebrate my strengths, which are English, drawing and music, and get help with math and physics. It turns out my math teacher has tutoring twice a week and there are a lot of kids in there! After going for three sessions, I'm finally starting to understand geometry! Ms. G also taught us to stop thinking negative thoughts, so I try to tell myself every day that I'm good at math. Sometimes that makes me giggle, and sometimes I find myself thinking I'm stupid again. It's hard, but I tell myself that I'm smart, not dumb, and I think I'm starting to believe it!

The most interesting thing happened in physics. Big D overheard me asking for help and offered to tutor me for free! He is so smart! He was at that talk last month too and I can tell he's lost weight, but even better, he smiles now.

We've studied together 4 times, and not only have I learned a ton, but I really like his company. He asked me to go on a bike ride this weekend and I said yes! Oh, and by the way, I found out his real name is Douglas.

Maddy smiled and waved at me in class today. I'm not sure why she did that, but I smiled back. Maddy has been my idol since we were in elementary school, and I always thought she lived a perfect life. Seeing her at the weight loss talk and now, noticing she's lost a little weight, I realize her life wasn't perfect and she needed change too. Ms. G warned us not to compare ourselves to others, to celebrate our strengths and to treat each other with respect, because no one is free from struggle. You never know, she said, behind a bright smile might be a world of pain. I will try to be that person to make a difference and smile back!

Ms. G

Working with the counseling department at Edison High School the past few months has been very rewarding but also a bit sad. These kids are energetic and smart and have amazing futures ahead of them. On the surface they appeared confident and successful, but as I got to know many of them, I noticed the common themes of poor body image, self-doubt and a shocking lack of knowledge about how to eat healthy and get proper exercise. I was starting to give up hope that I could make a difference until, on my last day, I heard three students talking near the lunch room. I probably shouldn't have, but I stood around the corner and listened to what they were saying. I was so proud of them!

Maddy, Douglas and Jessica were talking about exercise and good food choices! I nearly fainted I was so happy! They were discussing how much to eat at meal times. Maddy commented that she learned a meal should fit in two cupped hands and since she and Douglas were bigger, they need more food than Jessica, who is very petite. Douglas mentioned he is learning to be OK with the fact that he towers above most kids and how mountain biking three or four times a week is helping him lose weight and feel good about himself. He talked about the fact that self-esteem should be based on who you are and not how you look. I noticed Jessica's hair wasn't in her face as usual and she wasn't wearing that oversized sweatshirt that hides her small frame. She seemed to talk with a hint of confidence and, if I'm not mistaken, I think she has a little crush on Douglas.

I am so very proud of these kids! I hope they continue to tackle their issues with confidence, find the courage to ask questions when they need help and to believe in themselves!

1. Eat
2. Move
3. Believe

Meal Suggestions

Here are two examples for a day of healthy eating. Remember, do your research and decide what works for **YOU**! Unless noted, a serving size is what is listed on the packaging. **YES, YOU SHOULD READ LABELS!**

Breakfast: Two eggs, toast with jam, banana, coffee ~ 400 calories
Snack: An apple and water ~ 90 calories
Lunch: Sandwich with turkey, cheese, lettuce, tomato, mayo and mustard and an iced tea ~ 400 calories
Snack: Handful of salted almonds and water ~ 120 calories
Dinner: Roasted chicken (4 oz.), white rice (1 cup), roasted broccoli (1 cup) ~ 430 calories

This is a great day, with approximately 1440 total calories, which would be perfect for Jessica or for Maddy on a light workout day.

Here's another suggestion, which would be good for Douglas:

Breakfast: Oatmeal with Greek yogurt (3/4 cup), blueberries and chocolate milk ~ 480 calories

Snack: Peanut butter (1 Tablespoon) with 6 crackers and water ~ 200 calories

Lunch: Ham and Swiss cheese sandwich with mayo and mustard, carrots, corn chips, flavored water ~ 550 calories

Snack: Hardboiled egg and grapes (1 cup) with water ~ 130 calories

Dinner: Pasta with 3 meatballs in red sauce, a salad tossed with oil and vinegar and a glass of milk ~ 630 calories

This is what a 2000 calorie day looks like. For some it seems like a lot of food, *but this is an example of what an active teen like Doug requires to stay healthy and maintain energy levels throughout the day!* Please remember the portion rule: two cupped hands hold a meal and one cupped hand holds a snack. These two examples are just that, **EXAMPLES!** Read labels, look up foods on a calorie app and get to know what they're made of, so you can build your own menus with healthy foods **you like!**

You might be thinking, this will take time and planning. **It does.** Make the decision to quit whining, stressing, ignoring and complaining about things you want to change and take the time to **SIMPLY DO SOMETHING ABOUT IT!**

To be clear, this is not a diet. This is a good way to live every day of your life that will result in a healthier, leaner, stronger **YOU!** Going on a diet is like putting yourself in **FOOD PRISON** and, let's face it, no one wants to be in prison. Think about it. The diet industry takes in billions of dollars annually, and there's always that great new diet on the horizon that people are willing to throw money at. **DON'T WASTE YOUR MONEY!** If diets really worked, why would we need more than one? Get off the diet train and just eat healthy, exercise and believe in yourself. It's free, it feels good and you don't have to walk around hungry all day with diet salad dressing in your bag. That stuff is nasty anyway. Switch to olive oil and balsamic glaze with a dash of salt and pepper. Yum!

Words to live by

- Forgive yourself
- Change is a process, not an event
- Set yourself up for success with thoughtful planning
- Eat breakfast
- Take the stairs
- Set goals and work toward them
- Eat fresh foods
- Food is the most abused anxiety drug; exercise is the most underutilized antidepressant
- Eat 5 times a day. It speeds up your metabolism
- Get rid of negative thoughts and replace them with ones that guarantee success
- Picture yourself the way you want to feel and look every day
- Learn from failure, but don't allow it to destroy you
- Stop complaining. It doesn't produce results
- Get enough rest and sleep
- Drink water
- A shake is not a meal, it's a shake
- Never compare yourself to anyone; you are unique
- Limit foods with chemicals and additives that have long names you can't pronounce
- Diet pills don't work and can be harmful
- Read labels and educate yourself; no one else can do it for you
- Educate family and friends and invite them to join you
- Life brings challenges and changes, work through them, find your new normal and carry on
- If you're coming home from the football game and everyone in the car is yelling for food and you find yourself in a drive thru with no good choices, order something small, enjoy it, then get over it! You can't be perfect all the time:)

All proceeds benefit charities like the Futuro Del Oro home building project. For almost 3 decades teams of youth and adults have traveled to the quiet colonias tucked away in the rugged hills overlooking the Playas de Tijuana, Mexico to build homes, hope, and relationships with the working poor families and the marginalized in these local neighborhoods. Over 175 homes have been built over the past 30 years and, with your help, we hope to build many more!

Made in the USA
Middletown, DE
10 March 2022